How to Develop PLCs for Singletons and Small Schools

Aaron Hansen

Solution Tree | Press
a division of
Solution Tree

555 North Morton Street
Bloomington, IN 47404
800.733.6786 (toll free) / 812.336.7700
FAX: 812.336.7790

email: info@solution-tree.com
solution-tree.com

Visit **go.solution-tree.com/PLCbooks** to download the reproducibles in this book.

Printed in the United States of America

19 18 17 16 15   1 2 3 4 5

Library of Congress Cataloging-in-Publication Data

Hansen, Aaron.

How to develop PLCs for singletons and small schools / by Aaron Hansen.

  pages cm. -- (Solutions)

Includes bibliographical references.

ISBN 978-1-942496-02-1 (perfect bound) 1. Professional learning communities--United States. 2. Small schools--United States. I. Title.

LB1731.H265 2015

370.71'10973--dc23

                            2015010077

Solution Tree
Jeffrey C. Jones, CEO
Edmund M. Ackerman, President

Solution Tree Press
President: Douglas M. Rife
Associate Acquisitions Editor: Kari Gillesse
Editorial Director: Lesley Bolton
Managing Production Editor: Caroline Weiss
Senior Production Editor: Christine Hood
Proofreader: Miranda Addonizio
Text and Cover Designer: Rian Anderson
Compositor: Abigail Bowen

Acknowledgments

Many friends and colleagues assisted and encouraged me in writing this book. My association with Rick and Becky DuFour helped to forge my beliefs about the collective power of educators. Little did I know that their invitation to collaboratively develop a presentation five years ago would spark the journey of writing this book. Equally important to this project was Claudia Wheatley. Her ability to see the potential in others has influenced my life more than once.

Special thanks goes to Bill Ferriter, Adam Young, and Héctor García for collaborating with me to build a presentation that served as a rough outline for the content of this book. Paul Farmer, Tim Brown, and Joseph Ianora also helped in various ways. Christine Hood and all of Solution Tree Press are amazingly talented at what they do.

Others who have profoundly impacted my thinking and encouraged me over the years include Bob Dolezal, Rebecca Murdock, Mike Mattos, Leslie James, the faculty of White Pine Middle School, and my colleagues at the Northeastern Nevada Regional Professional Development Program, who are truly world class.

My parents have been my first and best teachers of hard work, persistence, and faith. Finally, Shaleah E. Hansen is not only a brilliant editor but also my soulmate forever. Sidney, Anja, Coltrin, Jentri, and Eddie, when I count my many blessings, I count you first.

Visit **go.solution-tree.com/PLCbooks** to download the reproducibles in this book.

Table of Contents

About the Author

 **Aaron Hansen** is a nationally recognized presenter, consultant, and author who empowers teachers and leaders to transform their schools.

As principal, Aaron led the transformation of Nevada's White Pine Middle School (WPMS) into a nationally recognized, high-achieving school. Under Aaron's leadership, WPMS won many awards, including Title I Distinguished School, National Model School (2009–2012), and the only middle school in the country to be named Middle School of Distinction (2010) by the International Center for Leadership in Education. Aaron has been featured in many books, articles, and TV news stories, including ABC's *World News With Charles Gibson*, CNN's *American Morning*, Fox Network's *Fox and Friends*, and the BBC documentary *Jodie Marsh: Bullied*, all highlighting the changes Aaron led in transforming school culture and combating bullying. Aaron was named Nevada's Innovative Educator of the Year in 2009.

Aaron is a contributing author to *It's About Time: Planning Interventions and Extensions in Secondary School*. He also has worked with thousands of educators across North America and beyond, helping them improve their processes in PLCs, RTI, teacher and leader improvement, student and staff culture, and comprehensive school transformation. He is a leadership consultant with the Northeastern Nevada Regional Professional Development Program.

To learn more about Aaron's work, follow him on Twitter @Aaronhansen77.

To book Aaron Hansen for professional development, contact pd@solution-tree.com.

Introduction

"How does all of this professional learning community (PLC) stuff work when I'm the only one in my school who does what I do?" If you are thinking this, you are a singleton!

Band, choir, special education, art, auto mechanics, welding, physics, consumer science, reading, technology, psychology, speech, business, drama, dance, media, K–5 in a small school, . . . the list goes on and on. Whatever your unique craft, I'm here to tell you that there is a place for you in the PLC process.

Framing the Problem

Traditionally, principals and teachers attend a PLC at Work™ Institute, listen to a PLC turnaround story, or read one of the many books about this topic and immediately see the potential power that the PLC framework offers. They get it; working together achieves so much more than working alone. So, they jump in with both feet. They begin tearing down the walls of isolationism with the promise of a new day built on a collective vision that *all* students can learn at high levels.

They start by organizing collaborative teams. Mathematics teachers with mathematics teachers, science teachers with science teachers, language arts with language arts, the band teacher with . . . uh, well, hmm. Wait a minute! What about that band teacher?

A similar problem occurs in many small schools, which are full of singletons. According to the National Center for Education Statistics (2013), 25.4 percent of schools in the United States are rural schools. Not all rural schools are small; however, many of them are. In many of these small schools, grade-level teachers or subject teachers are singletons. For example, in a small elementary school, it isn't uncommon to have one teacher per grade level or even one teacher for multiple grade levels. In a small secondary school, there may be only one biology teacher, one algebra teacher, one English 9 teacher, and one world history teacher—singletons! These schools hear the PLC message, agree with it, and then stumble on the inevitable singleton questions: How do you build common assessments when you're the only one who teaches your subject or grade level? Can this really work for you? Yes, it can and does!

As schools of all sizes take the plunge and begin working toward becoming a true PLC, some of the most common questions include, With whom do our singleton teachers collaborate, and what do they collaborate about? These questions matter, and they are addressed in this book.

Making the Problem Worse

In a school's haste to begin the PLC process, it is often the case that singletons, like the band teacher, are left out or assigned to a team as an afterthought. Understandably, guiding coalitions—the principal and a few teacher leaders who are guiding the PLC work—often make the mistake of focusing only on subjects that have the pressure of high-stakes testing. Inadvertently, they marginalize singleton teachers and their importance to the school community by not being thoughtful about the roles singletons can play within this new collaborative culture. When this happens, it's not unusual for singleton teachers to become resistant to the process, because they feel it is a waste of their time—largely, because it is! Without direction or a clear personal purpose for meeting, PLC meetings for singletons wind up having no impact on their work. We can do better!

If you are a principal or part of a guiding coalition, good for you! By picking up this book, you are taking a step toward becoming better informed about how to include *all* of your teachers in the collaborative process in meaningful ways. You'll be better able to help your school develop a truly collaborative culture versus one that is collaborative in some areas and isolating in others.

If you are a teacher, good for you! You are likely a singleton who is looking for practical solutions for how you can participate meaningfully in the PLC process. You, like so many others, probably know the power of collaboration but don't see how you fit into that process in your school. If you have felt marginalized in some way, I want to challenge you to assume good intentions. It is highly unlikely that your principal, and those working with him or her to help establish the PLC framework, thought, "Let's see how we can make some people feel devalued." Instead, assume that they just didn't know how to include you—yet. By picking up this book, you are empowering yourself with knowledge of how you too can collaborate in meaningful ways for the purpose of improving your craft and responding to student learning, either through supporting your current team structure or by proposing a new structure that works better.

This resource describes five different ways that teams can be organized for helping singletons and small schools participate fully in the PLC process.

1. Vertical teams

2. Interdisciplinary teams

3. Singletons who support

4. Virtual teams

5. Structural change

I have chosen to highlight these five methods for structuring teams because they are proven to work and address most situations. The scenarios presented illustrate ways in which teachers have found common ground for creating assessments and participating in the full PLC process. However, each school and each singleton situation has its own unique DNA. That is, it would be impossible to address every particular situation. However, using the principles in this book and your own expertise, you will be empowered to customize a collaboration solution. There is a solution for every teacher!

Avoiding "Collaboration Lite"

Mike Schmoker (2004) writes:

> Mere collegiality won't cut it. Even discussions about curricular issues or popular strategies *can feel good* but go nowhere. The right image to embrace is of a group of teachers who meet regularly to share, refine, and *assess* the impact of lessons and strategies continuously to help increasing numbers of students learn at higher levels. (p. 48, emphasis added)

The PLC process focuses on data, usually collected from common formative assessments. If a team is going to take seriously the charge of answering the following four fundamental questions (DuFour & Eaker, 1998), assessment becomes key.

1. What do we expect students to learn (know and do)?

2. How will we know if students are learning?

3. How will we respond when some students *are not* learning?

4. How will we respond when students *are* learning?

Think about it. How can you respond to student learning (questions 3 and 4) if you don't know where students are in the learning process (question 2)? I would assert that teachers aren't quite clear in knowing what they expect students to learn (question 1) until they have described what students should be able to do and at what rigor level they need to perform when they have learned it. In other words, until you can create an assessment question, task, or prompt that describes exactly what students must be able to do to demonstrate proficiency, you are not yet clear on what you expect students to learn. As Richard DuFour, Rebecca DuFour, and Robert Eaker (2009) tell us, the linchpin is assessment.

Common formative assessments must inform learning. They should:

- Help teachers determine how well they are teaching a concept

- Support teachers in learning from each other the ways to improve their craft

- Inform teachers about which students need more time and support

- Inform teachers about which students need their learning extended

- Inform individual students about their position in the learning progression

Bottom line, if a team isn't administering common formative assessments, it is practicing "collaboration lite."

Don't get me wrong; any increased level of collaboration is a good thing, and you have to start somewhere. However, the ultimate goal is for singleton teachers, like all other teachers, to become part of the common assessment process. Like with any rule, there are a few exceptions, which are discussed later in the book. *These are exceptions.* Whether singleton teachers are part of a vertical team, an interdisciplinary team comprising multiple singletons, a virtual team, or a traditional team, the goal is for them to take an active role in gathering and using data from common assessments to improve their craft and promote student learning. Figure I.1 (page 6) shows a continuum summarizing the steps teams should consider when forming a successful collaborative team. Visit **go.solution-tree.com /PLCbooks** for a reproducible version of this figure.

To that end, this book is not focused on theory or research but on practical experiences of teachers and schools who have found ways to make collaboration work. It serves as a springboard to readers who are looking for ideas and principles that they can apply to their own situation. There are many ways to do this, and your solutions will be as unique as your singleton situations. For the conscientious educator,

As you form your team, use the following continuum as a guide to think through some of the steps you'll need to take. The goal is to achieve the level of collaboration at the bottom of the continuum.

> Establish a team (vertical, interdisciplinary, or virtual), or change structures so that you are no longer a singleton.

> Establish a time to meet.

> Identify target skills or content worthy of your attention. If improved, these skills will make an important difference for students.

> Develop a means for assessment (often through the use of a common rubric).

> Establish inter-rater reliability and develop an assessment schedule.

> Establish SMART goals.

> Determine some best-practice strategies for initial instruction.

> Administer common assessments with an agreed method for grading and reporting the data.

> Disaggregate data gathered from common formative assessments.

> Decide on individual and collective responses to fundamental questions 3 and 4 of the PLC process.

Figure I.1: Implementing a singleton collaborative team.

the moral imperative to ensure that students learn the essentials looms heavy. However, ten times the pressure of that weight is the exhilaration of seeing students in your charge become empowered with the skills necessary to achieve to the best of their ability academically, build a productive career, and succeed in both school and life. As you find ways to harness the potential and power of true collaboration, I wish you the best on your journey.

The promise of a new day awaits!

Chapter 1
Vertical Teams

Think "common denominator." A vertical team is a team of teachers who all teach the same subject but at different grade levels. They form a team and focus on the common skills that they are teaching.

The Scenario

One of the most inspirational school turnaround stories I know is that of Bluff Elementary School in Utah. Situated in the breathtaking Southwestern Red Rock County of the Four Corners area, Bluff Elementary serves about one hundred K–5 students. Most of these students live on the Navajo Nation Reservation and are not native English speakers. Eighty-seven percent of the students receive free or reduced lunch. Many ride a bus seventy miles, thirty-five of them on dirt roads, just to get to school. More than 50 percent of the students are considered homeless by national standards. The challenges are immense.

The school had been designated a turnaround school by the state of Utah due to poor student achievement. Newly appointed principal Barbara Silversmith, along with a few of her staff, attended a PLC at Work Institute. They quickly agreed that the means by which they would turn around their school was through the PLC model. Mrs. Silversmith and her team had barely begun when they faced the singleton challenge. Because the school was so small, there was only one teacher per grade level. They asked, "This whole PLC thing is about collaborating with others who teach the same subject or grade level that we do. Who do *we* collaborate with? The nearest neighboring school is more than fifty miles away!"

Their solution was to organize into two teams by grade levels: one K-1-2 team and one 3-4-5 team. They dove in without time to spare, answering the first of the four fundamental questions: What do we expect students to learn (know and do)? Before the school year started, teams hung poster paper around the library walls, and they began posting on sticky notes the essential standards students needed to meet to be successful on the state test and, more importantly, in life. As they pored over state standards, the fifth-grade teacher provided input to the fourth-grade teacher, the fourth-grade teacher provided input to the third-grade teacher, and so on. Over the course of numerous discussions, the teams articulated essential standards and learning targets, and even talked about rigor levels for each grade.

The next question to address was: How do we build common assessments when we teach different grade levels? Learning from others who had experienced similar challenges in small schools, Mrs. Silversmith asked the K-1-2 team, "What skills at each grade level do you have in common?" The teachers didn't quite understand the question. She rephrased, "What *skills* are you working on in kindergarten that you are still working on in second grade?" The teachers referred to their language arts charts and found that many of the skills they were teaching spiraled up the grade levels. They listed the skills: reading fluently, learning vocabulary, comprehending texts, summarizing stories, summarizing informational text, making predictions, asking questions related to the text, writing complete sentences, recognizing text features, and so on. They had more in common than they thought! Through conversation and reviewing state, district, and school data, they determined that a common foundational skill with which students were struggling was writing complete sentences. They had determined a starting place.

The K-1-2 team discussed how many students at each grade level, particularly English learners (ELs), struggled to write complete sentences. With excitement, the team began seeing the commonality in their students' struggles, despite the fact that these students were of different grade levels and ages. The teachers built a simple star rubric for assessing complete sentences, as shown in figure 1.1.

I wrote some letters or words.

I wrote a simple sentence with a noun and a verb.

My sentence has a noun, a verb, and correct capitalization, spacing, and a punctuation mark.

My sentence is about one topic using a noun, a verb, and an adjective or elaboration. I used a capital letter, spacing, and punctuation.

My sentence is about one topic, using a noun, a verb, and an adjective. I used a capital letter, spacing, and punctuation. I used correct grammar, including tenses, pronouns, and so on.

Figure 1.1: Sentence rubric.

The learning target for a kindergartener was to produce a two-star sentence, while the target for a second grader was to produce multiple five-star sentences. The team established inter-rater reliability by grading student work together and gathering example anchor papers at each level. These success criteria were published for the students, along with time frames for when students should be able to perform at the identified levels.

The teachers regularly assessed student progress and kept simple progress-monitoring charts for each student. When the K-1-2 team met, teachers used the data from their charts to discuss individual student progress, particularly for those who were struggling to achieve the learning target. The teachers then designed flexible interventions based on need, not grade level. Therefore, a kindergartner who was already performing at a three-star or four-star level might receive intervention from the first-grade teacher for the intervention period, along with any other students from kindergarten, first grade, or second grade who were also at that level. Conversely, the second grader who was at a two-star level would meet with other students who needed similar intervention, no matter what their grade levels. The teacher who was best equipped to provide that level of intervention would provide it. The team members engaged in rich discussions about strategies they were using, what was working, and what they still needed to learn to help students improve their sentence-writing skills.

By repeating this process over time with other essential skills, the school became an amazing PLC success story. It dramatically improved student learning and achievement and became a model for others to follow. You can read more about Bluff Elementary's story at http://allthingsplc.info under "Evidence of Effectiveness."

The Principles

By focusing on what they had in common versus what they didn't, the K-1-2 team members were able to experience rich and productive collaboration. They were part of a true PLC! They met regularly. They identified what they wanted students to learn and at what rigor levels. They determined how they would assess and gather formative data about student learning. And in true PLC fashion, they used the data for two fundamental purposes.

1. Improve professional practice.

2. Improve student learning.

Now, let's look at how this vertical team was able to achieve the first fundamental purpose for gathering data—improve professional practice—compared to a traditional team. In a larger traditional PLC, teams comprise anywhere from three to seven teachers who teach the same grade level or subject area. Team members administer a common assessment and share their students' results. The team talks about what worked well and what didn't. If one teacher's students are achieving at higher levels, the other teachers try to learn his or her methods for success so their students can do the same. If there are high levels of trust within the team, a teacher who doesn't achieve the desired results can discuss it with his or her teammates and receive constructive feedback about changing strategies. A high-functioning team shares strategies, models lessons for each other, and learns and tries new strategies together. Teachers improve their professional practice in practical ways by using their own student data as a means for collaboratively improving what they do.

In the vertical team situation, a similar conversation takes place. However, instead of comparing student progress across all second-grade classes, the team compares student progress with the learning targets set for each grade level. The targets are descriptions of what is proficient at each grade level, and they are obviously different for kindergarteners than they are for second graders.

In the case of the K-1-2, team, three different targets are established, one for each grade level. The first-grade teacher (let's call her Mary) now measures the progress of her students against the first-grade learning target, not the second-grade or kindergarten students. She then compares her students' progress toward their target to that of her colleagues' students' progress toward their own respective targets.

The professional improvement conversations are very productive. Almost all of Mary's first graders have reached, or nearly reached, their learning target. However, the second-grade teacher (let's call her Sharon) is having some trouble getting her students to reach their respective second-grade target. The ages of the students are close enough that Sharon could use similar strategies with her second graders that Mary is using with her first graders to achieve the desired results. In this case, Sharon must learn what Mary is doing. Table 1.1 shows the learning targets and actual levels for Mary's and Sharon's students.

Table 1.1: First-Grade and Second-Grade Learning Targets

Students	Mary's First-Grade Class Learning Target: 2.5	Student	Sharon's Second-Grade Class Learning Target: 3.5
Jose	2.5	Billy	3
Fred	3	Gabriella	2
Kendal	3	Frederica	2.5
Karen	2.5	Angel	2
Kali	2	Daren	2.5
Lenora	3.5	Cesar	3.5

Without the data, Sharon might never know that her second graders are struggling, nor would she know that Mary is a great resource for learning new strategies. If the team preassesses and formatively assesses along the way, the teachers can monitor student progress and share strategies that work at either grade level. Team members are able to improve their professional practice through comparing student data.

The second fundamental purpose for gathering data from a common assessment, and arguably the most important, is to use data formatively to respond to and improve student learning. The vertical teams at Bluff Elementary broke from many traditional structures to help their students. First, they created a culture of trust and collective responsibility in which students were not *my* students and *your* students but *our* students. They all took responsibility for learning by sharing students during intervention times, which is not typical in most large or even small schools. The teams determined who was most qualified to provide specific interventions. Sometimes *most qualified* depended on particular teacher-student relationships; sometimes it had more to do with the learning target at hand.

They also broke from the traditional grade-level groupings. The intervention groups were based on student needs, not grade level. In the example scenario, Mary, the first-grade teacher, seemed the most qualified to provide intervention for students under the 3.5 level. In a perfect world, Sharon would provide support as a co-teacher to Mary as she retaught the skill, thus observing Mary in action and learning from her. In many small schools, this level of vertical collaboration is quite possible if the school is creative in leveraging some of the support staff, counselors, principals, or parents. The logistics of a small-school schedule are usually not as complex as they might be in a larger school, making this level of teaming effective if the team is willing to examine some of the traditional structures, like schedules and use of staff. Structures are discussed in more detail in chapter 5.

The other ancillary benefit to the nature of most vertical teams in small schools is that everyone on the team is vested in student success. The first-grade teacher is vested in the second-grade students' success, because those were her students last year. She already invested her effort and love into them and wants to help them achieve at their highest level. The third-grade teacher wants the second-grade students to succeed, because those are going to be his students next year, and so on. In a secondary situation, a high school band teacher is vested in the success of middle school band students, because they will feed his or her program in the future.

Opportunities

The first opportunity that Bluff Elementary created for itself was to develop a visual aide. The grade-level learning goals charts helped Bluff Elementary team members determine which skills they had in common. It became even more apparent that their challenges were similar when they started assessing using the same rubric. The opportunity for collaboration around similar challenges was there! Although this was completely different than the traditional grade-level structure, the teams recognized that they could work smarter, sharing the load through flexible intervention groups based on need, not grade level. The vertical teams had a vested interest in the success of their colleagues, because often, their colleagues' students would become their own students the following year.

The teams also defined the rigor levels at which they expected students in each grade to learn the essential skills. Many schools go as far as deciding what they want students to know and be able to do, but they fail to determine the rigor level. For example, there is a big difference between knowing multiplication tables and being able to apply multiplication to real-world problem solving. Bluff Elementary defined what they wanted students to learn *and* at what rigor level in each grade. This kind of vertical articulation is powerful for any school.

Although the vertical teams in the scenario are from an elementary school, vertical teams at the secondary level can and do create common rubrics for measuring long-term learning of essential skills. By creating success criteria or rubrics that describe the target at each grade level, the teams more clearly articulate the learning progression a student must achieve for ultimate success, instead of just passing the current class. Imagine if the English department at each high school had common rubrics that described good writing in grades 9 through 12, even though the performance expectations on the rubric for a ninth grader would be different than for a twelfth grader. How powerful would that level of clarity and consistency be for students to track their progress over a four-year high school career?

This is exactly what the English team at Kingston High School in Western Washington has done. Although the school is large enough to staff at least two teachers per grade level, the English department chose to work as a vertical team. Teachers started by working specifically on synthesizing, an outcome they identified as essential. They built a common rubric for grades 9 through 12 that described various levels of proficiency. The expectations for each grade level are made clear to students. Students are empowered with these clear expectations, tracking their progress for four years through a writing portfolio. Teachers collect progress data and spend their PLC time collaborating on how to teach essential skills more effectively.

What about science? What if the science team at your high school chose to collaboratively work on the essential skill of using critical thinking or applying the scientific method to problem solving, and students had clearly articulated learning targets each year for four straight years? What kind of impact would that have on students' abilities as scientific thinkers?

Similarly, what if the mathematics department applied these principles of collaboration around essential skills, even though the levels of mathematics learning are different? What if the mathematics department worked collaboratively with the goal of improving problem solving in real-world situations and had a common scoring rubric for how students approach real-life problem solving? Even though the performance expectations on a common rubric would undoubtedly be different for a ninth grader in algebra than they would for a twelfth grader in calculus, students and teachers would discover a common path that progressively moved toward the ultimate goal.

Another example might be a vertical music team. A high school band teacher could team with the middle school band teachers. DuFour (2011) suggests that:

> [They could] agree on standards students should achieve at their various grade levels and how to assess whether or not their bands are achieving the standards. They could videotape performances or rehearsals to share with their teammates, jointly assess the strengths and weaknesses of the performance, and discuss ways to improve upon it. They could set SMART goals regarding the ratings their bands get in competitions or the number of students who qualify for distinction in the regional or state band, or the number of students who remain in band from eighth to ninth grade.

The same process could be applied to a vertical art or drama team, using common rubrics and portfolios as a means for assessing and gathering data.

The principle of a vertically articulated set of essential learning targets is powerful when contrasted with the curricular chaos that reigns in most schools. Vertical articulation isn't just for small schools or vertical teams. If any size school is able to create a sustained focus, as previously illustrated, students are much more likely to learn the enduring skills that are necessary for success.

Challenges

One of the obvious challenges of this model is that student performance levels are different. Because of this, it is impossible to compare data the same way that a traditional team of four fifth-grade teachers or four algebra 2 teachers might compare data. Instead, this model requires an increased level of clarity about which skills must be learned at each grade level and *at what rigor levels* students must learn them, so teachers can compare progress.

For classes in which the content is focused largely on progressive skills, like secondary mathematics, this model of collaboration is more difficult. Common skills are easier to track in a social studies team comprising multiple grade levels and different content. However, common skills between a geometry and algebra class, although doable, are less obvious.

In some vertical teams, the teacher at the highest grade level might feel as if he or she is always giving versus receiving. Sometimes, singleton teachers don't have anyone in their building or district who teaches the same content, even at a different grade level. There might be other teachers offering similar content at various grade levels, but they are at different schools, making it next to impossible to meet during regular school hours due to conflicting schedules. However, if distance is the only impediment to a vertical team organizing, this barrier can be overcome through virtual teaming, as discussed in chapter 4.

Recommendations

The Bluff Elementary K-1-2 team was wise to list all the standards that teachers wanted students to meet. By doing this, they established a visual of all the common skills among grade levels. It would be wise for schools that are considering vertical teams to list essential skills for each grade level. Once teams have listed these skills, they can begin by selecting one skill to focus on as a collaborative team.

Often, schools feel pressure to improve quickly, and they try to do too much too soon. In the case of the PLC process, it is usually better to slow down in order to go faster. What I mean by this is if teams can experience the process successfully once, they will develop capacity to more easily repeat the process with other skills in the future. The process for a vertical team should look something like this.

1. List all the skills taught at each grade level.

2. Choose a common essential skill that is a priority for your team to improve. (Focus on skills that are most important to students' future success in your content area and life in general.)

3. Create a means for assessing students' progress (typically, a rubric).

4. Set age- or grade-level-appropriate targets for each grade level.

5. Preassess and share data.

6. Share, learn, and study best practices.

7. Formatively assess regularly, and talk about student progress, sharing ideas for in-class interventions and learning various ways to improve professional practice.

8. Respond to student learning collectively, if possible (share students if by doing so you can more efficiently and effectively meet student needs).

9. Reassess to evaluate the impact of your PLC process.

Teams that commit to following this process, and do it well with one essential skill, usually see great results and become committed to following the process with other skills.

Chapter 2
Interdisciplinary Teams

Interdisciplinary teams are groups of teachers who all teach different content but work together to develop common assessments around universal essential skills. By focusing on the *skills* that they are teaching, teachers can build common assessments despite the vast differences in their content disciplines. Upon closer examination, it is likely that they have more in common than they think. Again, think "common denominator."

The Scenarios

Interdisciplinary teams come in all shapes and sizes. This flexible model can and does work for a variety of teacher teams, such as foreign language teachers, music teachers, art teachers, social studies teachers, school-to-career teachers, and more.

Scenario 1

The North Orange County Regional Occupational Program (NOCROP) is an excellent example of effective interdisciplinary collaborative teams. NOCROP is a cooperative among five districts to provide quality instructors in the school-to-career arena. In short, the organization (not unlike other similar organizations in California) is contracted by more than twenty high schools to recruit, hire, and supervise teachers from various industries, such as culinary, welding, firefighting science, auto mechanics, computer-aided drafting, graphic design, hospitality, floral design, stage craft technology, film, banking, photography, American Sign Language (ASL), professional dance, and so on. The organization not only recruits professionals from various fields to become teachers through a state alternative certification program but also provides professional development to these nontraditional teachers. When asked, Terri Giamarino, assistant superintendent of NOCROP, explained, "The best thing we can do for our teachers, particularly our new teachers, is to help them develop true collaborative relationships with colleagues and be part of a team" (T. Giamarino, personal communication, December 1, 2014).

NOCROP's attempts to create meaningful collaborative teams have not been without challenges. One of its first challenges was providing regular times for teachers, who teach across multiple districts, to meet. They now meet once per month. The second challenge was structuring the teams. Who collaborates with whom? Terri and her team, with the support of Paul Farmer, a PLC associate, determined that they would organize teams under industry sector headings, which include:

- Agriculture, hospitality, tourism, and recreation
- Arts, media, and entertainment
- Building and construction trades/engineering
- Business and marketing
- Education, child development, and family services
- Health sciences and medical technology
- Public safety services
- Transportation

Some of the teams teach similar curricula, but most curricula are vastly different. For example, in the building and construction trades/engineering team, one teacher teaches carpentry, one teaches construction occupations, one teaches design, one teaches fabrication for engineering, one teaches computer-aided drafting, one teaches welding, and one teaches wood manufacturing. Each of these teachers is a singleton, part of a large interdisciplinary team.

Terri and her team's next singleton challenge was answering the question, What do our teachers collaborate about when most of them don't share common curricula? These school-to-career teachers found a common denominator when they examined their fundamental mission, which in part was "to help all students succeed in employment and career advancement" (NOCROP, 2015). The answer was clear—employability skills! Many of the students NOCROP serves choose their classes because they are driven to pursue their dream jobs right out of high school, or they want to get a head start on further education for a career. However, what good does it do a student to become a certificated welder if he or she doesn't know how to properly fill out a job application, write a résumé, conduct a successful interview, work with others, or take direction from a boss? Students' dreams of getting great jobs or starting careers are all for naught without employability skills. The first of the four fundamental questions focuses on what students must learn. What is more essential than employability skills?

So, the NOCROP teachers decided to focus on employability skills. Using the California Career Technical Education Model Curriculum Standards (California Department of Education, n.d.) and their own experience within their fields, they determined what skills were most essential for *all* students to learn, no matter what content they were teaching. The team settled on interviewing skills, résumé writing, and introduction letter writing as a good place to start. The teachers built common rubrics and began administering common formative assessments. Figure 2.1 (page 22) shows a portion of a common rubric the team developed.

Scoring Criteria	Exemplary 4	Proficient 3	Progressing 2	Beginning 1
First Impression/ Introduction	All from proficient, plus: • Genuine smile • Interested and enthusiastic	• Appropriate greeting • Firm handshake	• Weak handshake • Poor posture • Minimal eye contact • Weak smile	• No handshake • Late for interview appointment • No eye contact
Appearance and Poise	All from proficient, plus: • Confident body language	• Business attire, clean and pressed • Good hygiene • Good posture • Minimal makeup and jewelry	• Wrinkled clothing • Poor posture • Acceptable hygiene • Either underdressed or overdressed	• Inappropriate attire • Poor hygiene • Excessive makeup or visible piercings
Personal Attributes	All from proficient, plus: • Provided a specific personal example demonstrating award criteria • Explained why the skill or personal quality is important	• Asked questions • Asked for a business card	• Somewhat shy or nervous • Seemed interested • No questions, could be better prepared	• Extremely shy or nervous • Passive or indifferent

Figure. 2.1: Portion of NOCROP rubric for interviews.

One of those assessments was a performance assessment. Students participated in mock interviews with real employers from their fields of interest. Teachers tracked their students' progress over time, meeting monthly in collaborative teams to offer support and share teaching strategies and intervention ideas.

Despite the vast differences in content, the interdisciplinary teams were able to find a common denominator and improve the life chances of students, some of whom were considered at risk. They helped students live their dreams by achieving their goals and obtaining jobs with good salaries, when they otherwise may not have had the skills to do so. Terri explained that sometimes the work is slower than she would like, and a few of her teachers are resistant to the process. Overall, however, most of her teachers are excited that they now have a team with whom to engage in meaningful work. NOCROP continues to track the impact of its work. Visit www .nocrop.us to read more about this organization.

Scenario 2

Let's take a look at another typical scenario. Imagine you have just become part of a social studies team at a small, traditional high school. Your team has three members. You teach world history, while another member teaches U.S. history, and another teaches government. The content of each of these courses is completely different. There are some obvious overlaps, but largely, the content varies substantially. You want to fully participate in the collaborative process, but you aren't really sure how to proceed. You might have conversations about some of the obvious similarities, but how do you get to the level of collaboration for creating common assessments? What does a common assessment look like when the content is so different?

Think "skills." What are the intended *skills* each teacher on the team wants his or her students to learn? This is where your team must find common ground. After reviewing the state standards, you might list a few skills such as analyzing primary documents, summarizing, making and defending an argument in writing, comparing and contrasting the past to the present, comprehending maps and diagrams, comparing authors' points of view, researching, evaluating claims, learning vocabulary, and so on (National Governors Association Center for Best Practices [NGA] & Council of Chief State School Officers [CCSSO], 2010). None of these skills are specific to the content of world history, U.S. history, or government, but each skill is crucial to student success in any social studies class.

After listing the common skills, your team collectively decides to focus on making and defending an argument in writing. What would be your next steps? You might decide to read professional journals to determine, as a group, what a good argument looks like. You might decide to attend a workshop or consult with the English team for ideas. Early in the process, your team might develop a rubric that describes levels of proficiency at each grade level, much like Bluff Elementary did in chapter 1. You might find models of student work that represent various levels of proficiency on the rubric, so inter-rater reliability could be established among teachers as they score student work. The same models might be used as examples for students to clarify the learning targets. Your team might develop a series of common assessments (not specific to course content) to measure student progress. In short, once your team is empowered with a mindset to place student skills at the center of the collaborative process, you are ready to work. You are then ready to begin the process of answering the four fundamental questions.

The Principles

When interdisciplinary teams are getting started, they should consider what skills they have in common. Sometimes, team members who are engrossed in their content areas might tend to think about their own content first. This is a common trap. A teacher might think, "What does welding have to do with wood manufacturing? My content is completely different!" Naturally, the differences in content lead to discussions about what the team does *not* have in common. However, if the team focuses on the big-picture skills, as did the NOCROP and fictitious social studies teams, teachers likely will find that they have essential learning in common.

NOCROP is a particularly powerful example of an interdisciplinary team that is improving results for students in significant ways by focusing on essential common skills. Through review of the standards and discussions based on previous experiences as working professionals, it determined that employability skills were as essential as skills come. Given that the very purpose of its program is to help students launch into the world of work or down a career path, it just made sense to focus on the soft skills that are important to getting a job and being successful. Once the focus was established, rubrics could be developed, and the process of assessing and gathering data to monitor and respond to student progress was possible. To reiterate, it all began with identifying the essential common skills.

The fictitious social studies team also focused on skills. However, teachers focused on skills that were more directly linked to students becoming successful in their disciplines. The team assessed students' progress in those skills. When interdisciplinary teams are established, the more closely disciplines are linked, and the easier it is to identify common skills.

Teachers who are members of both of these teams still teach and assess their content, even though they are focused collaboratively on broader skills.

Opportunities

One of the many benefits of collaborating in interdisciplinary teams is that they must focus on skills. In the example of the social studies team, a content expert like a U.S. history teacher might get caught up in content-specific goals, deciding that every date, event, or recitation of minute facts is essential to the learning experience.

I'm not saying that content isn't important and U.S. history teachers should abandon content for skills only. Nor am I suggesting that the teacher not assess student learning of key points in the content. What I am suggesting is that the content becomes a vehicle teachers can use to teach skills. In today's knowledge economy, with information so readily available, remembering facts or dates is far less vital than the skills of evaluating large amounts of informational text, analyzing primary sources, making a claim, and supporting it with evidence. These skills are more suited to the demands of the 21st century. By working as an interdisciplinary team, members are forced to think more about relevant skills than isolated knowledge. When interdisciplinary teams ask the fundamental question, "What do we expect students to learn (know and do)?," the emphasis should be on *do*.

That said, in a perfect world, the U.S. history teacher would get together a few times a year with other U.S. history teachers to determine the essential content for their discipline. Even though this teacher's primary collaborative team would be interdisciplinary, he or she should ensure that key content curriculum is aligned with other U.S. history experts' key content curricula.

Examples

An interdisciplinary team comprising foreign language teachers might determine that one of its most essential skills is vocabulary acquisition. Even though the content is obviously different (various languages), the skills on which teachers focus as a means for acquiring the new languages are similar. These team members could collect data, share successful pedagogical strategies, and ultimately learn from each other about how better to teach their content.

Adam Young, a PLC associate and choir teacher, participated on an interdisciplinary music team that focused on sight reading (among other items) as an essential skill. The team developed a short sight reading preassessment in $^6/_8$ time for which students simply had to clap the rhythms. The team collected preassessment data, determined some common strategies, formatively assessed progress, revised strategies, provided feedback to students, and then conducted an end-of-semester assessment. Collaboratively, the teachers dramatically improved their students' abilities in this skill, which is essential to all musicians, whether they sing or play an instrument in the marching band, jazz band, or orchestra.

An interdisciplinary art team at Lowry High School in Nevada focuses its efforts on essential art elements, regardless of the medium students are using. Teachers developed common rubrics for assessing student work, which are universal enough to be used whether students are sculpting a ceramic sculpture or painting an oil painting. Students use the same rubrics all four years to track their work and reflect on their progress as artists in the essential skills.

Tim Brown, PLC associate and former principal, relates the story of a group of physical education teachers, counselors, and other singletons who came together as an interdisciplinary team to focus on study skills. Using these skills, this team wanted to impact a specific group of struggling students. The team members were able to clarify expectations, how they would assess (even though they didn't administer common assessments) and track progress, and how they would respond to students who continued to struggle. Their plan succeeded for nearly all of the students originally identified as at risk of failure (T. Brown, personal communication, March 1, 2011).

Another example is Del Amigo High School, a small alternative high school in California with about 60–120 students. Teachers meet weekly as an interdisciplinary team to discuss student progress. Their common denominator is students. The small faculty shares interest in every student who comes through its doors. With the help of the school counselor, every student has an individual learning plan designed to meet his or her specific skill needs. Principal Joe Ianora, who is also a PLC associate, explains, "We talk about what seems to be working for students in one class and if it is replicable in another. We review the plans and make sure students are on track with their goals. We discuss how we can improve our practice to help them develop essential skills, and we talk about what additional support they need" (J. Ianora, personal communication, December 20, 2014). Sometimes that support comes in the form of helping credit-deficient students make the connection between their success in school and future success. The team regularly leverages relationships it has built in the community through organizations, such as the Rotary Club, to help students get jobs in their chosen fields. Teachers gather plenty of data, even though they don't administer common assessments in the traditional way. These data are specific to each student's needs, and the team uses those data to meet those needs and to improve professional practice.

Challenges

One of the distinct disadvantages of organizing only in interdisciplinary teams is that teachers don't have anyone knowledgeable about their subjects with whom to discuss the content to be taught. This leads to teachers making content decisions in isolation. Interdisciplinary teams are usually focused on skills. If possible, teachers who are part of an interdisciplinary team should also meet occasionally with other teachers in the same discipline to ensure that their content choices are in line with others'.

Usually, the first challenge of an interdisciplinary team is determining what teachers have in common. It is typical for the team to first focus on the differences, such as, "You teach welding. I teach woodshop. The content is different." Team members must be willing to determine not only the skills that they have in common but also those skills they have not traditionally taught within their subject area. For example, a welding teacher may not even have employability skills on his or her radar. And even after identifying the significance of these skills, it may take some persuasion to help convince him or her that teaching them is worthy of his or her time.

Recommendations

As previously emphasized, the first task an interdisciplinary team should accomplish is to determine the essential skills students need to learn. I recommend that teachers first list those skills individually, drawing from their own experiences and state standards. When they compare their lists, they will begin to see the common ground. Then, through consensus, they can determine which of these common skills are most enduring or most important to students' future success. From there, the team must determine a means for assessing student progress in learning these skills by developing common rubrics and common assessments. At this point, teachers should establish some age-appropriate learning targets, similar to the Bluff Elementary example in chapter 1. Finally, the team must develop inter-rater reliability for using the rubrics or scoring assessments so that team members are accurately assessing students' progress. The interdisciplinary team can then function just like any other collaborative team.

Chapter 3
Singletons Who Support

Sometimes being part of a team means having to put the needs of others ahead of your own. When singletons support, they join a traditional team and support team goals, even when those goals have nothing to do with singleton content. Singletons who support can be very powerful! For this model to work, however, singletons who support must understand their role and be willing to support the goals the team sets, even when those goals don't have a direct connection to their content.

The Scenario

"Momma T."—that's what everyone calls her. She is the drama teacher at the small high school where I began my teaching career more years ago than I like to admit to myself. Mrs. Tucker (aka "Momma T.") stands five feet, one inch tall, but her vivacious personality is through the roof! Her drama classes and club put on some truly world-class performances in the small high school gymacafetorium (room that serves as a gymnasium, cafeteria, and auditorium in many small schools across the United States). Her hilarious stories usually have people in stitches, crying, or both within minutes of meeting her. One of her many talents is her ability to connect with students and build positive relationships. When students are struggling with life in general, a teacher, a counselor, or an administrator can bring them to Momma T. She will figuratively (and sometimes literally) wrap an arm around them, find a role or job for them to do, and help them feel like they have a place in the world. (She should have her own spot on the school's pyramid of interventions that just says, "Momma T.") She is one of those truly special people in the world that makes others around her feel special.

She, along with the computer teacher and media specialist, joined our English teacher team, which previously consisted of three English teachers who had worked together successfully for two years. No one provided direction on how to include these three singletons in our work, but they were joining our team. Needless to say, the team welcomed Momma T. with open arms, but we had to establish new norms so that Momma T. didn't lead us off on one of her funny stories or down a rabbit hole. No one had any idea about Momma T.'s or the other singletons' roles as part of the English team, but we were soon to find out.

In one of our first team meetings, the other two English teachers and I were discussing in what area we wanted to focus and create a SMART goal. We dominated the conversation, while the new singleton members remained quiet. The English team finally settled on the goal of improving grammar. Not that grammar was the most essential of skills we taught, but state assessment data showed that this was a huge weakness among our rural students. And as English teachers, we felt we needed to learn more about best practices in teaching grammar. It was settled. Grammar would be our starting place for the semester. Momma T. piped up without solicitation and said, "I can get behind that goal. For our students to get good jobs, keep those jobs, and generally be successful in life, they need to be able to speak and write well using correct grammar." I don't think the group thought much of the comment. We agreed and moved on.

A couple of weeks later, I vividly remember reviewing a grammar lesson at the board that I had taught just the day before. I was lecturing to my freshman class, which included a number of "rough" characters. You can probably guess how that was going, because lecturing at the board to the best of fourteen-year-old students about parts of speech is a poor strategy, let alone with a group that is typically less than attentive. Trying to push through, I turned to face the class, when a hand shot up from the back of the room. It was one of my students, Desiree. "Yes, Desiree?" She placed her hand on her hip, cocked her head to one side, and looked up. "That's not how Momma T. showed us how to do it!" Surprised and curious, I held the whiteboard marker out to her. "Okay, let's see how Momma T. showed you how to do it." She marched right up to the board and demonstrated Momma T.'s strategy for the class. I stood, stunned, for a few moments, trying to figure out what just happened. Desiree, of all people, was correcting my grammar on the board in front of the class!

A few days later, I sat in my team meeting, dying to ask Mrs. Tucker about the strategies she was using with her drama students. "Momma T., you have to tell me how you're teaching your students parts of speech, because Desiree stood up in my class—" Momma T. explained, "Well Aaron, here's what I'm doing. When we read scripts in class, I tell students, when you get to this adverb, I want you to move like *this*. When you hit this pronoun, I want you to *belt it out*! Although this reflexive pronoun is written like this, I want you to say it like *this*." I listened intently as Momma T. explained how she taught a subject that students hated in my classes and usually cared nothing about. Instead, she taught grammar within the context of a subject that they loved and cared deeply about. I marveled at her power! Because the students loved her and loved what she loved, Momma T. was able to help them learn the targeted skill. Our team then started exploring integrated approaches to teaching grammar. I do not exaggerate when I say that I believe Momma T. had a greater impact on the team reaching its SMART goal that year than I did, because, as she said, "I can get behind that goal."

The Principles

Successful singletons who support must recognize that their role is exactly what it sounds like, to support. They must be willing to support the goals of the core team as their own, recognizing either the universal connection of the essential skill to their own content or the overall importance of that skill for student achievement. Momma T. was willing to get behind the team's SMART goal, because she understood and believed in the value of the goal for student success, even though it wasn't directly connected to her drama curriculum goals. Singletons who support effectively often have to step completely outside of their content area, but they are willing to do so as part of a team focused on an important common goal. They take a stance. They realize that being part of a community sometimes means putting the greater good before their own priorities. Sometimes, however, singletons who support also have personal learning networks (PLNs) that they regularly access for content-related ideas and improvement, which is discussed in chapter 4.

When singletons join a team, it's best if there is an obvious connection between the content area of the team and the content of the singleton. A middle school technology teacher or media specialist whose curriculum focuses on using modern tools to conduct viable research, such as software and apps, could easily join a language arts, science, or social studies team. For example, imagine that the science team has determined that it is essential for students to understand how to apply the scientific method. The science teachers typically have students conduct multiple short research projects, or mini experiments, and then give short, in-class presentations. Meanwhile, the technology teacher expects his or her students to learn how to use technology tools to conduct viable research and present their new skills in presentation programs and applications. The science team's priority is applying the scientific method. The technology teacher's primary focus is learning presentation tools and skills. This situation presents an excellent opportunity not only for the singleton to support but also for the team to mutually support one another.

The team can develop a common rubric focused on science while incorporating the use of new technology tools. Team members can support each other as they help their students work toward mastery of these important skills, as opposed to having students work on isolated, unconnected projects. The extra time and support from different content classes helps students make relevant connections among subjects they are learning. The science team benefits, because they have a technology, research, and presentation expert among them. That allows the science teachers to focus their time on science content. The technology teacher, and specific skills learned in technology class, will undoubtedly help students produce a better final presentation in their science class. Students might even research science topics in technology class. Even though the science teachers benefit most in this support scenario, the technology teacher definitely receives something in return. She has the support of a whole team, helping to reinforce the importance of skills learned in technology class. The technology teacher also has a team to help with intervention when the time comes.

Another example is a special education teacher (sometimes called *inclusion teacher* or *co-teacher*), especially one in a school practicing inclusion. This teacher can be a powerful singleton who supports. Although the special education teacher doesn't bring data from his or her own class to the team meeting, he or she should be engaged with the team in disaggregating the data, deciding on in-class interventions and Tier 2 collective response interventions that the team provides.

In a true co-teaching situation, co-teachers should act as one when they meet with their team. An effective special education teacher brings an extra level of expertise in pedagogy, providing a unique perspective and knowledge about student learning modalities. He or she is involved in planning meetings and then takes the learning targets the team is planning to teach and scaffolds them in a way to help all students learn better during initial instruction (Buffum & Mattos, 2014). For example, in regard to vocabulary, imagine that a fifth-grade team is teaching a unit on the layers of the Earth. Working backward, the team reviews the common assessment to be used after the unit. The special education teacher looks specifically at one question:

What is the outermost layer of the Earth?

    A.   Crust

    B.   Mantle

    C.   Core

    D.   None of the above

He or she recognizes that students not only will have to learn the content vocabulary *crust, mantle*, and *core,* but also will have to understand the meaning of *outermost.* By creating a secondary vocabulary list, this teacher is able to support students with learning disabilities or language deficits, as well as help the rest of the team be intentional about direct instruction. This way, the team can better plan with *all* students' needs in mind.

The special education teacher in a support role doesn't necessarily determine the content to be taught; however, he or she can help the team determine the best way for students to access the content the first time. By including the special education teacher in planning sessions, the team has a fresh set of eyes to help anticipate students' initial challenges. Often, this teacher reviews the content that is planned and is able to identify one or two students he or she knows will struggle. These efforts often end up benefiting the whole class. A popular analogy is that of a wheelchair ramp. A school may build a wheelchair ramp so a specific student with a disability can access his or her classroom. However, many other students also will use the ramp as they enter the classroom. Although the special education teacher may design vocabulary maps or provide other scaffolds for a few individual students, those same scaffolds likely will benefit many students. For this kind of initial support, the special education teacher must be in the planning session and understand that this is part of his or her role on the team.

When the team assesses and reviews its data, the special education teacher should be involved. He or she can work with the team to determine specific learning deficits of all the students, and then the team can provide appropriate and targeted interventions, not just pull out students with individualized education plans (IEPs; see Buffum & Mattos, 2014, chapter 2).

Schools regularly make the mistake of assigning a special education teacher to participate in three or four different grade-level teams, which is not practical. Often, these teams meet at the same time, making it impossible for the special education teacher to truly be part of each team or attend regularly. Even if the teams meet at different times, the special education teacher usually gets spread so thin that he or she can do little to contribute to the success of any team. It is best if the special education teacher works with one or maybe two grade levels or department teams, at most.

Counselors also are often singletons who support. Because of the role the counselor usually plays, he or she may be assigned to meet with multiple teams. The counselor's role is to meet with the teams about specific students who are struggling with problems or conditions that might impede academic progress. Because the counselor meets with multiple teams, he or she needs to have a schedule of regular meeting times. The team should know ahead of time which day the counselor will attend the team meeting. The team should be prepared to share specific concerns about students who are struggling with issues that fit within the counselor's role. When the counselor has a specific role in supporting the team, it provides an avenue for better understanding students' needs and challenges. He or she can work on those needs with students and their parents or refer students to the Student Support Team (Buffum, Mattos, & Weber, 2012). The counselor also can provide the team with strategies for helping students who might be struggling with behavior or academics. He or she can observe classes objectively to help diagnose why specific students are struggling and provide strategies for teachers to support hard-to-reach kids. The counselor assists the team by helping to determine any challenges students may have that are impeding their learning. Counselors can be powerful singletons who support if they know their role and teams utilize their expertise and resources.

In larger schools, counselors can form their own counselor team, setting SMART goals based on attendance, reducing bad behaviors, increasing good behaviors, increasing scholarships earned, discussing case scenarios, or anything that supports the organization's goals. They can track data to observe the impact of specific strategies and as a means for informing and improving their practice.

Some singletons are called on to support by providing time for grade-level teams to meet. Elementary schools often use specials teachers, such as music teachers, library media specialists, or physical education teachers, in their master schedules as a means for creating time for regular teachers to meet or to provide common intervention periods. Although this is not ideal for singleton teachers, it may be the only way a school can manage to provide time for teams to do this important work. When this is the case, it is essential to recognize the significance of this gift of time (a four-letter word in most schools)! There is never enough time in schools. When singletons are asked to relieve this burden of time for their peers, they are offering a huge contribution to the learning community. We need to do a better job of recognizing and celebrating that contribution. When employing this strategy, it doesn't mean that specials teachers don't also collaborate with the team in support of team SMART goals, but they likely won't meet with them every week. Singletons in this type of support role should have the opportunity to collaborate on a rotation, through calendared days or by some other means, so they can support team learning goals and improve their craft through interactions with peers.

DuFour (2008) writes about media specialists in this kind of scenario:

> We will continue to recommend that these professionals (media specialists) teach children and that they can be scheduled to do so in ways that contribute to making time for their colleagues to collaborate. We will also continue to stress that the school schedule and calendar should provide time for the library media specialist to work directly and regularly with the teams of teachers as important contributors to the collaborative process.

Opportunities

Sometimes the only reason some students might come to school is because of an elective class or an activity they love. Sometimes it's because they love the teacher. Sometimes they love a particular subject or class. Sometimes they love a subject because they love the teacher, and the teacher loves the subject. Our singletons are often the Momma T.s—those teachers who provide kids with a place in the world and a passion that keeps them coming back to school. Teachers like Momma T. are invaluable to school culture because of the amazing difference they make in the lives of students. However, too often those teachers are placed on teams as an afterthought, with little to no direction. They get frustrated, and rightfully so, because they don't see any application to working collaboratively with a team that doesn't have anything to do with the content area for which they are so passionate.

However, these talented folks can have a tremendous impact and, as Momma T. said, "get behind" worthy goals. In this case, Momma T. understood and believed in the importance of students speaking and writing well and using proper grammar. Because she saw the goal as an enduring skill, she was able to work as part of the English team and support the team goal. She helped students see that grammar had some relevance to a subject that they loved. She showed the English teachers a better way to teach through an integrated approach, so that students actually remembered. She influenced both student and adult learning. However, Momma T.'s decision to get behind the team goal was hers. Little had been done to help her see what her role could be. She figured it out on her own. A more effective team would have helped her, and a guiding coalition should have explained how the roles could or should work.

Challenges

Had Momma T. not supported the English team's goal, neither the team nor the students would have benefited from her contributions. Arguably, she has a strong enough personality that she could perhaps have even partially derailed the team from functioning well at all and inhibited them in achieving their goal altogether.

In this story, I mentioned that the media specialist and computer teacher also were assigned to the team. Although neither of them was resistant, they did not make a choice to become vested like Momma T. did. They didn't see the vision of the greater good with enough clarity to get behind the goal and make a difference. Subsequently, their impact was minimal at best, and they often reported feeling like they had better things to do than meet with the English teachers.

A large part of collaborative team success is mutual accountability. Most schools do not provide a way to hold singletons who support accountable for results like they do with nonsingletons. In a traditional team, like a mathematics team, accountability is embedded in the process, because each mathematics teacher administers common assessments and shares the results. Because teachers share their results with each other, there is a high degree of peer accountability to do what the team decides. Even if a mathematics teacher doesn't believe in the process, he or she is still accountable. (Hopefully, through experience, such a teacher begins to see the value of collaboration.) In the case of the English team and Momma T. as a singleton who supports, the common assessment was administered in English classes only. The team didn't bother to measure Momma T.'s impact with actual results. That was a mistake. Because we didn't measure her results, the team didn't really hold Momma T. accountable for supporting the goal. We just took her word for it. Had the team thought a little more deeply, Momma T.'s students' scores on common assessments could have been compared to the rest of the students' scores. The team could have analyzed the impact of her instruction against what students received in just English classes. By doing so, the team could have held her and the other singletons accountable and also better celebrated her influence. In addition, we could have brainstormed ideas with those who were struggling to see how they could meaningfully support the team's goal.

If a singleton who supports is going to have an impact as part of a traditional team, he or she must take a vested interest in the established goals and understand his or her role in achieving those goals. Placing singletons on a team as an afterthought, hoping they will figure out how to participate in a meaningful way, is not a viable option and is doing a disservice to those teachers and their teams.

Recommendations

Perhaps the best place to start with recommendations for this chapter is to describe what *not* to do. Principals and leadership teams should not assign teachers as an afterthought. They should not place singletons on a traditional team without providing direction about the singletons' roles. Guiding coalitions should think specifically about the strengths of team members and the content connections that a singleton teacher may bring to a traditional team. That being said, if you are a singleton and are placed on a team without direction, do not assume it was done with bad intentions or even neglect. It is highly unlikely that your principal or the guiding coalition of your school placed you on a team with the intent of leaving you floundering and confused about your role. The more likely scenario is that your principal is figuring this out as he or she goes. So, if you are a singleton in a support position who feels undervalued at the moment, choose not be offended. Instead, the lesson from both perspectives is, assume good intentions and keep communicating until everyone is clear about the role of team members in the process.

Just like the strategies previously outlined in this book, this strategy may work for some but not others. It would be unlikely for every singleton teacher to join a traditional team and feel like the team's goal was a worthy pursuit. However, many singletons can, as Momma T. did, get behind worthy goals, even if these goals aren't connected to their own content. And sometimes, whether or not it feels like it is worth the effort, the team may need their support. Sometimes, putting the needs of others in front of one's own is exactly what being part of a team and a community is all about. Most teachers are all about contributing to the greater good, if given the chance. So, don't choose to be offended if someone asks you for support. Instead, choose to be honored that you've been asked to contribute to the greater good. You have something to offer, and that's being recognized!

That said, it is rare for guiding coalitions or traditional teams to actually have a conversation with singletons called on to support. Naturally, singletons in this situation might feel like they were placed on the team as an afterthought. Those teachers often report feeling undervalued and might consider the effort a waste of time. If a school is going to employ the singletons who support strategy, an honest conversation must take place about what the role of the singleton can and should be—first, with the singleton and then, with the whole team. Learning how the team can work together honors those involved and establishes the best chance for success. Using this chapter as a collective study is a good place to start that conversation. Nevertheless, if you are a counselor, a special education teacher, a drama teacher, or any singleton who supports, and you want your role to become more like what is described in this chapter, it may be up to you to define that role. Don't wait for your principal to fix your team or your team to magically see your value. Leadership is about action, not position. Momma T. led our team to discover a more integrated approach to teaching grammar by committing to the team goal and doing her best to support it. She not only impacted student learning, but also influenced the rest of the team to change strategies. She had a tremendous impact on the team and continued to contribute as the team moved on to other goals. You can do the same!

When forming teams, principals and guiding coalitions must consider numerous factors beyond the obvious grade levels or subject areas. They should think about individual strengths, weaknesses, personalities, content knowledge, and how the curriculum of their subject areas connect with others.

When a principal approaches a singleton to be part of a team in a support role, he or she should engage the singleton in an authentic conversation honoring his or her thoughts and ideas for supporting the team. The principal might say something like this: "Hi, Debbie. Thanks for letting me visit with you today. I know you are aware of our schoolwide efforts to work collaboratively to improve student learning. As we look at how to include everyone in this effort, it gets a little tricky with some teachers, like you, who is the only teacher teaching in your subject area—CNA classes. After considering it for a while, I think what makes the most sense is for you to work with the health team. I think there are some similarities between your curricula, and you can help support each other. However, sometimes, the team will be working on issues that really don't apply to your curriculum, so you would just have to be willing to support teachers in their efforts. I know you have a lot of experience and knowledge to share. How do you feel about working with them? Will you be able to support the team's goals? (Listen to her response.) Thanks, Debbie. I really appreciate what you do and *will* do to help your team reach its goals. I also really appreciate you being willing to be a team player. I know you are going to provide a lot of support to this team. Let's go visit with your team, so members know what your role will be in this effort."

Singletons who are already in the support role or who want to support a team might consider how their contributions could help the team reach their goals, and then share their thoughts. For example, "I was thinking about our goal. I think I could really help students by doing _____ in my classes. What do you think?"

Singletons who support can be powerful additions to collaborative teams in a PLC. Each situation in which a singleton joins a team in the support role will be unique. The role the singleton plays as the team strives to reach its goals also will be unique. In order for teams to capitalize on the potential contributions that singletons can offer, the singleton must be able to get behind the goals, and everyone on the team must understand his or her role.

Chapter 4
Virtual Teams

Welcome to the 21st century! Virtual teams provide a way for singleton teachers to no longer be singletons. By using technology readily accessible to almost anyone, singleton teachers can find others who do exactly what they do and meet virtually to do the work of a collaborative team, regardless of where they live. It just takes a little tech savviness, a strong commitment, and other people who are just as committed. Districts can help teachers who teach the same content at different schools to form virtual teams. However, prospective virtualists, beware—it isn't as easy as you think.

The Scenario

Casey Rutherford was the only physics teacher in his Minnesota high school for seven years. When the district developed the expectation that every teacher would participate in a collaborative team, Casey was excited about the prospect of working with peers but quickly realized he was a singleton. However, Casey had an advantage. He was an avid Twitter user who had amassed a large PLN, including close to two hundred physics teachers! Casey decided to find out if there were others in his PLN, like him, who wanted to become more structured in learning together. He pitched his idea to his supervisor to make sure he would be meeting the district's expectations. Then he sent out a tweet: "Anyone interested in using student work to collaborate about physics instruction? If so, click here." The link led to the following short invitation on a Google Doc (Rutherford, 2013):

> My name is Casey Rutherford. I am entering teaching for the eighth year, my seventh teaching physics and my first using modeling instruction (a specific approach to teaching physics). I have a relatively odd request.
>
> My school is implementing PLCs, certainly a worthy task. The problem is that at this point, there is not a logical person with whom I could form a PLC. Thus, my request. I am wondering if any of you would like to form an online PLC with me, working together approximately 30 minutes/week to compare student work. My thought is that we can do a lot with formative assessments, using photos of student whiteboards to form the basis for our conversations. I am, however, open to other ideas as well. I also am very interested in standards-based grading.

Casey was overwhelmed with initial responses from close to a dozen people! After a few trial-and-error meetings in which attendance was spotty, six physics teachers agreed that the only way this was going to work was if they made the commitment to attend regularly. The team's first norm was established. It committed to meet virtually via video conferencing in Google Hangouts on Thursday evenings and bring student work to share. Casey's virtual PLC was born!

In a way, the team was very diverse. Casey, along with two other teachers, came from traditional public high schools in Minnesota, Iowa, and Pennsylvania. One teacher taught at a charter school in upstate New York. The other two members taught at wealthy private schools, one in Delaware and the other in New York City. Although the settings in which the teachers taught and student backgrounds were diverse, Casey found his ideal team. Each team member was teaching physics at an advanced placement (AP) level and focused on a specific approach to teaching physics called *modeling instruction*, which gave him or her common resources to use. Additionally, team members were either practicing or interested in adopting standards-based grading. By casting a wide net over his PLN, Casey was able to find colleagues who were doing exactly what he was doing.

Once the team committed to meet regularly, it quickly developed a common formative assessment for a unit on constant velocity motion. Right away, it became clear that in spite of the diversity of their school settings, kids were kids. The team observed similar mistakes in student work and were able to brainstorm ways for reteaching. Casey's team used information gathered from analyzing student work to improve professional practice and respond to student learning. In short, Casey's team became a high-functioning virtual PLC!

The Principles

The traditional work of a collaborative team is not bound by location. Using modern tools for communication, teams can meet via video conferencing, share documents, and engage in the same conversations they would have if the meetings were taking place face to face.

Researchers estimate that more than one-third of all Americans are now meeting their spouses online (Cacioppo, Cacioppo, Gonzaga, Ogburn, & VanderWeele, 2013). Given the seemingly endless connectivity of people through social networking sites, it's not much of a stretch to think about forming a teacher team online.

Another advantage for Casey and his team was that they were all fairly tech savvy. So, using Google Apps did not create a steep learning curve for any of the team members. Using Google Hangouts, team members were able to video conference with each other. Using Google Forms and Docs, the team was able to share documents, such as assignments, quizzes, and tests. Again, using these tools is not complicated, and they are free. However, an initial time investment is required in order to become familiar with the technology and applications. Many technology tools and platforms are available, in addition to Google, which make collaboration much easier. Some quick examples include GoToMeeting, WebEx, Adobe Connect, and Skype, just to name a few.

Opportunities

Casey's team was able to work together like a typical teacher team. The team met regularly, using the four fundamental questions as a means for guiding its collaborative work. In that sense, its work was not unique. What makes Casey's story unique is that he did not let being a singleton within the walls of his school deter him from finding others in the same situation. Using readily available technology tools, Casey was able to find others with similar interests and build a high-functioning team. This opportunity is available to anyone with the will to make it happen.

Casey took advantage of having already developed a powerful PLN in which he was learning and sharing with others. The social/professional networking service Twitter is a perfect place to find others with similar interests. The service is free and easy to use. Once a user has established a username and password, he or she can start searching for colleagues, just like Casey did with other physics teachers.

Casey explained that the professional relationships he developed have been one of the great benefits of reaching out to form a teacher team. When on a trip to New York for vacation, he arranged to have coffee with one of his teammates. With another teammate, he co-presented at a national physics conference, and they modeled a lesson together. For Casey, and potentially many others like him, these professional relationships transform their professional practice.

Challenges

Although Casey's team's example is both exciting and inspiring, developing a virtual teacher team isn't always a simple and straightforward process. A common challenge faced by teachers when forming a virtual team is finding peers to begin with. Not everyone is going to have an established PLN over which to cast his or her net, like Casey. Casey had already spent a couple years developing his PLN. For those who don't already have a network, they will have to make an effort to start building a network, connect with existing networks, or find another means for connecting with others who do what they do.

In a traditional and successful PLC, meeting with one's team is simply an expectation of being a teacher in that school. Along with these expectations, time is provided during contract hours for teachers to meet regularly. The administration holds teams accountable for meeting and participating in the work, and the principal has the same expectations for all collaborative teams. There is a level of clarity about the work established, simply from being in the same school, sitting in the same meetings, and having the same leadership. When a singleton tries to form a virtual team individually, most of those conditions don't exist. First, the team often has to meet outside of school hours, because finding a common prep time is next to impossible. Because team members must meet on their own time, they must be very committed to each other and make it a priority to meet regularly. Otherwise, life gets in the way. Without accountability from the school or a supervisor, team members must be disciplined and committed to showing up and abiding by agreed-on team expectations and norms.

Virtual teams need strong leaders. When traditional teams are in their infancy, they often go through growing pains to figure out what the work should be and how to use their time most effectively. Virtual teams are no different. When a traditional team struggles to find its feet, usually people, such as the principal, an instructional coach, or another team, is in the building to turn to for guidance. The coach may come to a team meeting and help the team get back on track. A virtual team usually doesn't have the same kind of support, although it could. Team members are often on their own, meeting outside of school hours. They must provide their own leadership. The team must be truly committed and intrinsically motivated to meet and willing to hold each other accountable, because in most cases, it is unlikely that every team member has the same external motivation to participate. The flip side of this challenge is that these teams can be very strong, because they have chosen to participate and commit themselves to the process.

Recommendations

Even though the work of a virtual team in a PLC is the same as a face-to-face team, and technology tools make finding and communicating with colleagues easier, building a successful and productive virtual team has its challenges. However, if you're intentional in your planning and execution, it can be done. The following recommendations can help you with implementing the process.

Find Other Teachers in Your Discipline

Although Twitter isn't the only source for finding people, it is a great one! This social and professional networking service allows users to search for other users with similar interests. Twitter even makes suggestions to users about who they might be interested in connecting with. Many readers are undoubtedly already long-time Twitter users. However, if you are not a current Twitter user, a great place for a new user to start is to read the following blog post by William Ferriter (2011): "Electronic Teaming for Singletons in a PLC." Ferriter also has posted tutorials for using Twitter to find other singletons with similar interests.

Besides Twitter, singletons could certainly use other social networking tools, such as LinkedIn, Facebook, Pinterest, or others, the same way they would use Twitter. If Twitter or one of the other networking services just isn't your thing, you could definitely rely on word of mouth. Just start asking around. It is likely that you will quickly find someone who knows another teacher in a neighboring district who teaches your subject. Singleton teachers also could reach out to regional professional development organizations within their state or state departments of education as a resource for finding others in their content area.

Clearly Communicate Your Intentions

Once you find other teachers in your content area, follow Casey's example by explaining your wishes and intent, and invite others to join you. It is likely that if you find a large enough network over which to cast your net, like Casey did with his PLN, you will find a number of potential team members. While describing your intent, be as specific as possible, explaining what level of commitment you're looking for from your team and what kind of work you would like to do. For example, you might say, "I'm looking for potential team-mates who are willing to meet every two weeks to do the following: determine what students need to learn and at what rigor levels, work with me to develop and administer common assessments, and ana-lyze data from those assessments for the purpose of improving our teaching strategies and skills and responding to student learning."

By being clear, you will weed out those who just want to "collab-orate lite." Casey also was able to home in on those who had very similar interests. He found colleagues who were teaching AP physics, using the same specific approach (modeling instruction), and who were interested in standards-based grading.

Make a Pitch to Your Supervisor

If you're a singleton in a situation like Casey, in which the district expects every teacher to participate in a collaborative team, you prob-ably will be placed on an interdisciplinary team or assigned as a sin-gleton who supports. These scenarios were discussed in chapters 2 and 3, respectively, and can be very powerful and meaningful experiences. However, if you're passionate about the virtual team process and would strongly prefer to engage with others who teach in your content area, consider how you might approach your supervisor for support. How will you obtain support in forming a virtual team? Likely, if there is a school or districtwide initiative, there will be a means by which the principal is holding teams accountable. The teams likely are required to submit agendas or team action record forms. If not, you can show your commitment to the virtual team process by bringing along a team action record form to the appointment with your supervisor.

A team action record form is a tool for setting the team meeting agenda and recording what is accomplished during the meeting. This form might include the following information.

- Team name
- Date and time of meeting
- Team members present and absent
- Team SMART goal
- Meeting agenda
- Critical points for discussion
- Follow-up actions and who is responsible for those actions
- Date and time of next meeting
- Agenda for next meeting

Visit **go.solution-tree.com/PLCbooks** for a reproducible version of a team action record form.

Your meeting might go something like this: "I'm very committed to the PLC process. I get it! I want to engage in the process, but I want to participate by meeting with other teachers who teach what I teach in my content area. So, here's what I'm thinking. I would like to form a virtual team with other (fill in the blank) teachers outside of our school. The work that we do will be the exact same work that a traditional team does—determine what must be learned, create and administer assessments, analyze assessment data, improve instruction, and so on. Each time I meet with my team electronically, I will fill out this form and submit it to you so that you know I'm using the time productively. In fact, if you would like to attend any of the meetings, that would be great! What do you think? Can you support me in this?"

As a former principal, I can't imagine getting in the way of committed staff members who have a good plan, as long as they follow through with their promises.

Decide on the Logistics

Once you've garnered the support of your supervisor and reached out and found committed teammates, now what? You must decide on the logistics. When will you meet? What electronic platform will the team use for conferencing and sharing documents? From there, your team will do the same work of any collaborative team, such as setting norms for behaviors, developing SMART goals, and generally following the processes outlined in *Learning by Doing* (DuFour, DuFour, Eaker, & Many, 2010). The virtual team leader, however, will have a few more responsibilities compared to a typical team leader. He or she must manage the creation and distribution of meeting links and invitations and manage products in shared files where all team members can access them.

District Virtual PLCs for Singletons

Another typical scenario for using virtual PLCs is within a district. Before inviting people from different school sites to start collaborating with tech tools, allow them to give you some recommendations. For example, imagine that you are the district director in charge of music in your district. You have three high schools in your district, each with a band program. The distance between these schools makes it impossible for the three band teachers to meet in person on a biweekly basis during the time provided by the district, like the other collaborative teams. In the past, you've been able to squeeze a few hours out of district training time in August and January to get the three directors together. They have responded positively, but it hasn't been enough time, and it hasn't been regular enough for true collaboration. You think, "Could we meet virtually?" The answer is yes!

Setup for Success

Be sure you think through how you will set up this team for success. What would you need to do? Following are some requirements.

- Make sure team members have a common time within their day to meet. (This may require you to work with principals on changing teacher schedules in at least one of the schools.)

- Meet with the teachers to explain the purpose of their participation in the PLC—for example, the four fundamental questions. Develop a shared vision for what the work will look like for that team in their subject area.

- Develop strong norms. (If you think you have seen disengaged adults in face-to-face meetings, wait until they are alone with a computer and can, with the click of a mouse, be doing anything but participating.)

- Make sure team members have technology that works and that any district filters or Internet blocks aren't inhibiting the applications or software they will use to hold their meetings.

- Make sure that teachers have basic technology competencies and appropriate training in the programs or applications they will use.

These logistics are critical to setting up a team for success and avoiding the obstacles that might otherwise exist without them.

Leadership and Accountability

Because these teachers don't report directly to you but to their principals, think through the accountability and schoolwide obligations that might arise at each school. It is important for all principals to understand what their band teachers are doing, so they can be supportive and uniform in their expectations for the team's work. If one principal asks all the teams in his or her school to produce common unit assessments for the first quarter, and another principal asks all of his or her teams to develop their responses for when students are struggling, team members could be receiving mixed messages from different sources regarding what needs to be accomplished. Previously, I suggested that singletons approach their supervisor with some sort of team action record form as a means for keeping administrators informed about their team's work. The same should be done in this situation. For administrators to be able to support and celebrate the work of team members on their faculty, they need to know what's happening in their teams.

District Virtual PLCs for Small Schools

A small school with one teacher per grade level could form grade-level teams virtually with a sister school. This way, a first-grade teacher could meet with other first-grade teachers. The challenge is that the schools might be very different. In this scenario, a guiding coalition should be formed, comprising the principal from each school and key leaders from various grade levels from both schools. The coalition must articulate decisions as a coalition versus decisions at each school site.

Because resources, such as staffing, schedules, and interventions, differ at each site, the way teams respond when students are not learning likely will be different. Student demographics might also differ. By working through the four fundamental questions, the teams can determine what they expect students to learn. They can develop common assessments, assess their students, and use the data collected to improve professional practice. However, how they respond to student learning is more difficult to decide collectively. That likely will vary from school to school. Individual teachers might gather ideas about how to intervene, but beyond that initial Tier 1 response, the interventions applied are determined by the intervention systems in place at each school, available staff, schedules, and so on.

A multischool guiding coalition helps guide the work of teams, creating clear expectations along the way. The key here is that principals truly commit to the decisions made in the guiding coalition. Let me illustrate why that's important. Imagine Principal Smith tells her teachers that preparing agendas before a meeting is crucial to the work and holds her teachers accountable for submitting them. Principal Jones believes that the work is an organic process and developing and sticking to agendas doesn't really matter. Therefore, he does not hold his teachers accountable for creating or submitting agendas. When a teacher from Principal Jones's school does not develop an agenda, the teacher from Principal Smith's school becomes frustrated, fearing that Principal Smith will hold her accountable for not meeting expectations. She might feel that her colleague from Principal Jones's school is either slacking or that they are being held to a different standard—because they are! Imagine the possible conflicts from there.

Because two cultures are melded in a multischool collaborative team, it is crucial that the multischool coalition meets regularly to help guide the work and do its best to establish consistent expectations. The coalition must develop a mission, a vision, and strong, collective commitments to guide its work. One of those commitments should be consistency when decisions are made at a multischool level.

Just as with the band teacher example, participants must have working technology and know how to access and use it effectively. All of the other conditions, such as schedules and filters, must exist here as well.

The possibilities are endless for collaborating with peers through technology. Distance doesn't matter. The technology really does make it easy to find and communicate with others in your field. The challenges are human related. The biggest of these is getting everyone on the same page with the same expectations for what the work is and how to do it, despite different contexts. That is, and always will be, the greatest challenge of collaborating, virtually or face to face.

Chapter 5
Structural Change

Structures, or the ways schools are set up, create a context that promotes certain behaviors. Sometimes, schools might have traditional structures that promote isolation. If we examine some of those traditional structures, we often can change the context to encourage the human behaviors we desire, like collaboration.

Allow me to illustrate this concept with an overly simplistic analogy. Imagine you are in a crowded room in Denver, Colorado. You ask the group, "How many people here are proficient downhill skiers?" A number of hands would surely go up. Then, you ask how many people are proficient surfers. The number of hands would surely be fewer. Now, imagine you are transported to San Diego, California. You ask the same two questions about skiing and surfing. It's likely that the number of hands raised in response to those questions would be the opposite. The reason for this would be different contexts. The context, or environment, encourages different behaviors and hobbies.

Changing weather patterns is not likely a viable strategy for encouraging a change in people's behavior within schools. However, understanding that behaviors exist within certain contexts might help if we examine some of the traditional structures of our schools, such as schedules and room assignments. We might be able to change some of the context, which naturally encourages different behaviors, such as collaboration. Let's look at an example within a school.

The Scenario

I was asked to be the principal of Nevada's White Pine Middle School (WPMS), a small school with only 330 students and a structure of isolation. One teacher taught all the eighth-grade mathematics classes on one floor of the school. Another teacher taught all the seventh-grade mathematics classes on a separate floor, and a third teacher taught all the sixth-grade mathematics classes on the opposite side of the building. (This pattern was the same for each subject area.) All the mathematics teachers had different lunch periods, prep periods, and copy machines in close proximity to their rooms. In addition, no designated collaboration time was built into the schedule. How often did they collaborate? Never. Not because they didn't want to, but because they never saw each other! The context, or structure, did not support collaboration among teachers in content disciplines.

To become an effective PLC, the first goal was to answer PLC fundamental question 1: What do we expect students to learn (know and do)? Up until then, teachers rarely met as departments. No systemic attempt had been made to define essential learning. We began by changing one of the structures that was inhibiting departmental collaboration—location! We reassigned rooms, so departments were close to each other. We also changed the schedule, a major structure in secondary schools, so teachers had common preps and common lunches with their departments. Immediately, teachers began conversing with each other. Then, we developed a collaboration schedule. We engaged in serious curricular discussions about what needed to be learned at each grade level. The structure and context changed and, in turn, our behaviors also began to change.

As the staff learned more about the PLC process over the next year, we recognized that the current structure of one teacher teaching one grade level in his or her subject was keeping us from moving past collaboration lite. We knew we must find a way to administer common assessments if we were going to truly answer the PLC fundamental questions. The challenge was that every teacher was a singleton. How could we administer common assessments when no one taught common classes?

Through much conversation about how to best structure teams to meet our goals, we came to a consensus. We determined that we would change our structure, at least for a while, so each mathematics teacher taught at least one section at each grade level. The eighth-grade mathematics teacher would teach at least one section of sixth-, seventh-, and eighth-grade mathematics. The same was true for each core subject. Although we were apprehensive about the additional prep work, we committed to try the new structure. This way, we could have common formative assessments and all of the benefits that go with them. The structure of the master schedule changed.

The Principles

In many schools, the structures are arranged in opposition to collaboration, and most people will not work in opposition to the structures. Michael Fullan (2005) writes, "The truth is that the system changes individuals more often than individuals change the system" (p. 218). Here, Fullan refers to systems, which have a broader meaning than structures. Structures lie within and make up systems. However, the same conclusion applies.

Most people's behavior follows the established structures. If the structures promote isolation, most people will not resist those structures. Instead, they continue to be isolated, even if they continuously talk about collaboration. If we want to guide teachers out of isolation and into collaborating about common goals and assessment results, we must at least examine the existing structures. If we don't, teachers might be set up to fail. Creating structures that promote collaboration does not guarantee that teachers will collaborate; however, keeping structures that promote isolation makes creating a collaborative culture extremely difficult.

Structural changes must be intentionally designed around the behaviors we desire. WPMS wanted to collaborate in department teams because of curricular decisions that needed to be made. The primary purpose for the change was to answer PLC fundamental questions 1 and 2: What do we expect students to learn (know and do)? How will we know if they are learning? A structure of department teams was the best way for WPMS to begin answering those questions.

After much discussion, four years later, WPMS made a consensus decision to create a new hybrid structure in which teams met most of the time in grade-level teams and less frequently in subject teams. The primary reason for the change was because the focus of the work had shifted from answering PLC fundamental questions 1 and 2 to focusing on questions 3 and 4. By collaborating more often in grade-level teams, teachers discussed the students they shared. They were better able to improve their intervention systems and respond to students who were not learning or who required extended learning.

The point is, one structure is not inherently better than another, but it may promote one behavior, while a different structure may promote another. Schools must know what behaviors they want and realize that structures *can* change as they pursue different goals.

In presentations, I often share that you can tell when a secondary school is serious about learning for all instead of just saying that they are. The school changes its master schedule. The master schedule is a difficult structure to change, but schools put their money where it counts when they schedule opportunities for students to receive extra time and support within the school day. They become honest in their declarations when structures, like schedules, align with what they say is important.

Opportunities

In essence, in the WPMS scenario, singletons among core teachers were eliminated. Teachers were now able to design and administer common formative assessments. Teachers determined with greater clarity a vertical alignment of what students should learn at each grade level. In the past, teachers often blamed their students' deficiencies on the lower-grade teachers. (Sometimes, rightfully so.) "If the sixth-grade teacher would make sure students learned (fill in the blank), I wouldn't have to spend so much time reteaching it! No wonder my students are struggling with grade-level material." Now, whom do teachers have to hold accountable for students failing to learn essential content in previous grades? Themselves!

The master schedule, a major structure in secondary schools that largely dictates what people do, allowed teachers to share students. The schedule was designed so teachers often taught the same grade levels at the same time. This allowed them to combine classes or share students, so they could provide more targeted and fluid interventions.

Professional learning improved. A new or struggling teacher now had the support of a team that was teaching the exact same grade level. A veteran teacher was forced to re-examine a learning strategy that she had used for years when her colleague's students outperformed hers, using a different strategy. Teachers examined grading practices with the intent of creating a more consistent means for measuring student learning across staff and grade levels.

The school also experimented with looping, a strategy in which teachers have the opportunity to teach the same group of students the next year in order to truly recognize students' strengths and weaknesses and build long-term, meaningful relationships.

Both students and teachers gained an outlet for situations in which a personality conflict arose or a student was failing a class. In the old system, the student would have to stick it out, because there was only one eighth-grade science instructor, and the student needed eighth-grade science to move on to high school. If the student failed, the only option was to repeat the class with the same teacher, a prospect neither the teacher nor the student looked forward to. The new structure created more options.

Challenges

The most obvious disadvantage in this scenario was that teachers moved from preparing for one core class they repeated throughout the day to preparing for three. In addition, many core teachers in this small school also taught an elective and an advisory section. With advisory, some teachers ended up with five preps! Teachers often reported feeling overwhelmed with the preparation, like they were jacks-of-all-trades and masters of none. When preparing for so many different classes at a secondary level, at least one of them probably suffers.

Although time was set aside for meeting in grade levels to discuss interdisciplinary learning, it was limited because each teacher was a member of three grade-level teams. It was almost impossible to meet regularly in grade-level teams to discuss individual students struggling in all classes, whether it was an issue of behavior, effort, academics, or the need to revise an IEP.

Another challenge that secondary schools might face in changing structures so drastically is state certification requirements. Although Nevada allowed the structural changes described for WPMS, not all states will allow changes in all core subject areas, especially at the high school level.

Recommendations

Few schools are able to implement structural changes to the same degree illustrated in the WPMS scenario. However, many schools can improve collaboration by applying the principles on a smaller scale.

For example, many high schools, large and small, have identified freshman algebra 1 as their most important mathematics class, often called the "gate-keeper to college." Mathematics teachers and principals recognize that all freshmen must be proficient in these basic skills to graduate from high school and be prepared for postsecondary studies. So, instead of assigning this class to the least experienced teacher with the lowest seniority, like many schools do, they ensure that every teacher, even the calculus instructor, teaches at least one section of algebra 1. These schools engage in the collective process of identifying exactly what students must learn and how they know whether students are learning it. They develop collective responses for when students are not learning. In other words, they make sure that the collective experience and brilliance of the whole mathematics department is brought to bear when it comes to establishing this foundation. They settle for nothing less than making sure that for this most important class in their discipline, each student is successful. They take the same approach in other subjects as well.

However, teachers in some content areas, like science, have a more difficult time changing structures at this level because of state certifications. For example, a physics teacher might be the only one with a certification to teach physics.

Traditional structures in our schools can often get in the way of our goals. Sometimes, the only reason we can find for why these structures still exist is that it's always been done that way. By at least being willing to examine structures, we can assess whether they are beneficial or if there might be a better way to support our goals.

Epilogue

Milbrey McLaughlin stood in front the National Staff Development Council in 1995 and declared, "The most promising strategy for sustained substantive school improvement is building the capacity of school personnel to function as a professional learning community" (Many & Sparks-Many, 2014, p. 32). Twenty years after Milbrey's statement, I affirm her declaration, along with just about every organization, prominent researcher, and writer in education today. PLCs are still our best hope. Since 1995, the PLC process has proven to be exactly what she said it could be for so many schools and districts across North America and beyond.

However, I think it's worth pointing out what Milbrey did *not* say. And that is, "The most promising strategy is establishing PLCs . . . with the exception of singletons." Yet, this is what so many schools do! They fail to properly honor the teachers who don't teach subjects that are tested, or they assign these teachers to teams as an afterthought. Instead of creating a collaborative culture, they create a divided culture, thus negating much of its potential power.

On the other hand, some schools have tried to include their singletons, but they struggle to provide a clear vision of how singletons can contribute to the process or the work. Those singleton teachers may realize the potential power that Milbrey and others have described, but without support, they just don't know how they fit in. Therefore, they flounder.

My goals for writing this book are twofold. The first goal is to give hope to the many singleton teachers who want to engage in the worthy work of collaboration but don't know how. It is my hope that some of the examples I have shared, and the explanation of principles behind each scenario, have provided another path for singletons. It is also my hope that singleton teachers will be able to apply these principles as they develop strategies that are as unique as their own challenges. It is my hope that they will find ways to work with their colleagues to make even more of a difference in the lives of their students. I am excited to hear about the unique solutions singleton teachers develop!

My second goal is to help school leaders gain a better vision for how they can include *all* faculty members in this meaningful work. DuFour et al. (2010) state, "One of the great ironies in education is that it takes strong and effective leadership to create empowered people capable of sustaining improvement" (p. 192). By providing structures that promote collaboration and clarifying the roles that all teachers can play, including singletons and teachers in small schools, leaders can empower all teachers to engage in the collective and systematic inquiry of improving student learning. When that effort becomes a sustained effort, schools transform. It has been my privilege as a teacher, principal, and consultant to witness such transformations.

Margaret Mead's famous quote applies: "Never doubt that a small group of thoughtful committed citizens can change the world; indeed, it is the only thing that ever has" (as cited in Lutkehaus, 2008, p. 261). Let's make sure that this small group includes singleton teachers too. The promise of a new day awaits!

References and Resources

Buffum, A., & Mattos, M. (2014). *It's about time: Planning interventions and extensions in secondary school*. Bloomington, IN: Solution Tree Press.

Buffum, A., Mattos, M., & Weber, C. (2012). *Simplifying response to intervention: Four essential guiding principles*. Bloomington, IN: Solution Tree Press.

Cacioppo, J., Cacioppo, S., Gonzaga, G., Ogburn, E., & VanderWeele, T. (2013, June 18). Marital satisfaction and break-ups differ across on-line and off-line meeting venues. *Proceedings of the National Academy of Sciences of the United States of America*. Accessed at www.pnas.org/content/110/25/10135.full on February 1, 2015.

California Department of Education. (n.d.). *CTE model curriculum standards*. Accessed at www.cde.ca.gov/ci/ct/sf/ctemcstandards.asp on February 1, 2015.

DuFour, R. (2008, June 3). What is the role of the library media specialist in a professional learning community? [Web log post]. Accessed at www.allthingsplc.info/mobile/blog/view/31/what-is -the-role-of-the-library-media-specialist-in-a-professional-learning -community on February 1, 2015.

DuFour, R. (2011, November 30). How can elective teachers participate in the PLC process? [Web log post]. Accessed at www .allthingsplc.info/blog/view/154/how-can-elective-teachers -participate-in-the-plc-process on February 1, 2015.

DuFour, R., DuFour, R., & Eaker, R. (2009). New insights into professional learning communities at work. In M. Fullan (Ed.), *The challenge of change: Start school improvement now!* (2nd ed.) (pp. 87–104). Thousand Oaks, CA: Corwin Press.

DuFour, R., DuFour, R., Eaker, R., & Many, T. (2010). *Learning by doing: A handbook for professional learning communities at work* (2nd ed.). Bloomington, IN: Solution Tree Press.

DuFour, R., & Eaker, R. (1998). *Professional learning communities at work: Best practices for enhancing student achievement.* Bloomington, IN: Solution Tree Press.

Ferriter, W. M. (2010, November 2). Twitter for singletons [Web log post]. Accessed at http://digitallyspeaking.pbworks .com/w/page/33908410/Twitter%20for%20Singletons on February 1, 2015.

Ferriter, W. M. (2011, June 24). Electronic teaming for singletons in a PLC [Web log post]. Accessed at www.allthingsplc.info/blog /view/136/electronic-teaming-for-singletons-in-a-plc on February 1, 2015.

Fullan, M. (2005). Professional learning communities writ large. In R. DuFour, R. Eaker, & R. DuFour (Eds.), *On common ground: The power of professional learning communities* (pp. 209–223). Bloomington, IN: Solution Tree Press.

Lutkehaus, N. C. (2008). *Margaret Mead: The making of an American icon.* Princeton, NJ: Princeton University Press.

Many, T., & Sparks-Many, S. (2014). *Leverage: Using PLCs to promote lasting improvement in schools.* Thousand Oaks, CA: Corwin Press.

National Center for Education Statistics. (October, 2013). *Table 4. Number of city, suburban, town, and rural regular public elementary and secondary schools with membership and percentage distribution of students in membership, by state or jurisdiction: School year 2011–12.* Accessed at http://nces.ed.gov/pubs2013/2013441/ tables/table_04.asp on February 1, 2015.

National Governors Association Center for Best Practices & Council of Chief State School Officers. (2010). *Common Core State Standards for English language arts and literacy in history/social studies, science, and technical subjects.* Washington, DC: Authors. Accessed at www .corestandards.org/ELA-Literacy on February 1, 2015.

North Orange County Regional Occupational Program. (2014). *Employability skills rubrics.* Anaheim, CA: Author.

North Orange County Regional Occupational Program. (2015). *About North Orange County ROP.* Accessed at www.nocrop.us/about /default.html on February 1, 2015.

Rutherford, C. (2013, February 27). A physics PLC: Collaboration at a distance [Web log post]. Accessed at www.allthingsplc.info/blog /view/210/A+Physics+PLC%3A+Collaboration+at+a+Distance on February 1, 2015.

Schmoker, M. (2004, November). Start here for improving teaching and learning. *School Administrator, 61*(10), 48–49.

Solutions for Professional Learning Communities

The *Solutions Series* offers practitioners easy-to-implement recommendations on each book's topic—professional learning communities, digital classrooms, or modern learning. In a short, reader-friendly format, these how-to guides equip K–12 educators with the tools they need to take their school or district to the next level.

How to Use Digital Tools to Support Teachers in a PLC
William M. Ferriter
BKF675

How to Leverage PLCs for School Improvement
Sharon V. Kramer
BKF668

How to Coach Leadership in a PLC
Marc Johnson
BKF667

How to Develop PLCs for Singletons and Small Schools
Aaron Hansen
BKF676

How to Cultivate Collaboration in a PLC
Susan K. Sparks and Thomas W. Many
BKF678

How to Launch PLCs in Your District
W. Richard Smith
BKF665

"Tremendous, tremendous, tremendous!

The speaker made me do some very deep internal reflection about the **PLC process** and the personal responsibility I have in making the school improvement process work **for ALL kids.**"

—Marc Rodriguez, teacher effectiveness coach, Denver Public Schools, Colorado

PD Services

Our experts draw from decades of research and their own experiences to bring you practical strategies for building and sustaining a high-performing PLC. You can choose from a range of customizable services, from a one-day overview to a multiyear process.

Book your PLC PD today!
888.763.9045

Solution Tree